The Children's
Rhyming Bible

An imprint of Rose Publishing, Inc.
Carson, CA
www.Rose-Publishing.com

Contents

In the Beginning	5
The Forbidden Apple	7
Noah and the Flood	9
Father of a Nation	11
The Favorite Son	13
Strange Dreams	15
Reunited!	17
A Basket in the River	19
The Dreadful Lesson	21
A Path Through the Sea	23
Faithful Ruth	25
Samson, the Strong	27
The Shepherd Boy	29
Jonah and the Big Fish	31
In the Lions' Den	33
The Brave Queen	35
A Baby in a Stable	37
Following a Star	39
Fishing for Men	41
The Sermon on the Mount	43
The Lost Son	45
The Good Neighbor	47
The Healer	49
Five Loaves and Two Fish	51
Calming the Storm	53
A King's Welcome	55
The Betrayal	57
A Cross on a Hill	59
Jesus is Risen	61
Thomas Doubts	63
A Special Gift	65
Saul Sees the Light	67
Spreading the Good News	69
Letters of Love	71

RoseKidz® An imprint of Rose Publishing, Inc. 17909 Adria Maru Lane Carson, CA 90746 www.Rose-Publishing.com
RoseKidz® reorder# L50004 • ISBN10: 162862499X • ISBN13: 978-1-628624-99-1 • Juvenile Nonfiction/Religion/Christianity
Written by Courteney and Janice Emmerson-Hicks; illustrations by Anna Shuttlewood

The Children's
Rhyming Bible

Bible stories retold in verse by
Courteney & Janice Emmerson-Hicks
with illustrations by Anna Shuttlewood

In the Beginning

"Let there be light," said God at first,
When all around was dark.
He called light 'day', he called dark 'night',
And that was just the start.

He made the seas, the streams and lakes,
The plants and trees so green.
The moon and stars shone out at night,
By day the sun was seen.

He filled his world with birds and beasts
That swam and walked and flew:
With toads and tigers, goats and geese,
And mice and monkeys too.

Then God made man and woman both
To live in this new land.
And God was pleased with all he'd done,
With all that he had planned.

The Forbidden Apple

Now Eve and Adam both could eat
From any plant that grew,
Except the Tree of Knowledge,
Which God forbade them to.

The cunning snake told Eve to pick
An apple from the Tree.
"It will taste sweet," the serpent hissed,
Then watched her bite in glee.

Eve bit the juicy apple and
Then offered Adam some,
And straight away they realized
That they had nothing on!

They hid in shame but God still saw,
He knew they'd disobeyed.
Though sad, he clothed, then cast them out:
They could no longer stay.

Noah and the Flood

God knew that he must start afresh,
The world had lost its way.
So he would send a mighty flood
To wash the sin away.

Then Noah built a great big ark,
And to it there did come
All kinds of creatures, big and small,
A pair of every one.

For forty days and forty nights
They sheltered on the boat.
Deep water all around them lay,
But they stayed safe afloat.

But then the land was seen once more
And life could start again.
God put a rainbow in the sky:
A sign of hope for them.

Father of a Nation

Abraham had faith in God
And followed his command:
"Leave your home," God said to him,
"Your wealth, your flocks, your land."

Abraham did as he was told
And travelled far away.
God promised then to bless him and
His family one day.

"In time you will be father of
A nation great and strong.
Though you and Sarah are both old
One day you'll have a son.

"Your children will be like the stars
That twinkle in the sky:
So many you could never count,
No matter how you try."

The Favorite Son

Now Jacob had a dozen sons
But he loved Joseph best.
He gave a special coat to him,
And this annoyed the rest.

Then Joseph told his brothers of
Some strange dreams that he'd had.
They showed he'd rise above them all:
It made his brothers mad.

They sold him to a slaver and
To Egypt led the trail.
Things started well but all too soon
He ended up in jail.

Prisoners there spoke of their dreams.
He told them what they meant:
That one would die and one be saved.
Things happened as he said.

Strange Dreams

Great Pharaoh had a dreadful dream
Of skinny cows and grain.
When no one understood they sent
For Joseph to explain.

With God's help Joseph told him of
The future they foretold:
Seven years of plenty, then
A famine would unfold.

Then Pharaoh took off Joseph's chains
And put him in command.
Joseph stored the extra food
In barns throughout the land.

When famine came they were prepared
For they had been well led.
Their surplus lasted out the years,
And no one went unfed.

Reunited!

But back home things were not so good:
They'd nothing left to eat.
And Joseph's brothers had to go
To Egypt to buy wheat.

Joseph's brothers came but who
He was, they hadn't guessed.
He hoped they now were better men
And so he set a test.

So Joseph hid a silver cup
In his youngest brother's sack.
In the desert they were caught
And they were all brought back.

The other brothers pleaded then,
"Take us and spare the boy!"
Joseph knew that they had changed,
And hugged them, full of joy.

A Basket in the River

Poor baby Moses floated in
A basket made of reeds.
"All Hebrew boys must now be killed!"
Cruel Pharaoh had decreed.

But Pharaoh's daughter found him there
And saved him from the waves.
He grew up in the palace, but
The Hebrews were still slaves.

In later years he could not bear
The cruelty in the land.
He packed his bags and went away
But God had other plans:

"To Egypt you must now return
And tell the Pharaoh there,
That he must free the Hebrew slaves,
Or of my wrath beware!"

The Dreadful Lesson

Then Moses went to Pharaoh but
The king would not relent.
So God sent many dreadful plagues:
A message must be sent.

First the rivers flowed with blood
And all the fish did die.
Then frogs filled houses, gnats appeared
And flies blacked out the sky.

A plague on livestock, boils and hail,
Next locusts stripped the land,
Three days of darkness — all were bad,
But worse was now at hand.

All the first-born sons were killed
But Hebrews God did spare.
Pharaoh's son died too. In grief,
"Be gone!" he did declare.

A Path Through the Sea

So Moses led his people out,
But Pharaoh changed his mind,
And when the Hebrews reached the sea
His hordes were close behind.

The vast Red Sea was deep and wide
There was no way to cross.
With Pharaoh's army at their heels
They thought that all was lost.

God cleared a path to let them pass,
The waters held at bay.
But when the soldiers tried to cross
The waves washed them away.

Moses knew that God would always
Be there as their guide;
They swore to love and honor him
And he stayed by their side.

Faithful Ruth

Naomi's life was very hard,
Her sons and husband gone.
She loved her sons' wives very much
But longed to go back home.

She told the girls that they must stay
Though she would sorely grieve.
Then Orpah sadly said goodbye,
But Ruth refused to leave.

"Wherever you go so will I,
I won't leave you alone.
The God you love will be my God,
Your home will be my home."

Now Ruth worked hard to feed them both
Back home in Bethlehem.
She found a husband, bore a son,
For God looked after them.

Samson, the Strong

Fierce Samson was both big and strong,
No braver man was there.
To show that he belonged to God
He never cut his hair.

His enemy, the Philistines,
Soon learned to hate this man,
Who carried out attacks on them,
And fought throughout the land.

Now Samson loved Delilah, though
A Philistine was she.
She learned his strength lay in his hair,
And told his enemy.

They cut his hair, put him in chains,
But soon his hair grew back.
He pulled a temple down on them,
In this, his final act.

The Shepherd Boy

Young David was a shepherd boy,
He kept the wolves at bay.
He knew that God was by his side
No matter night or day.

Goliath was a warrior:
A giant fierce and strong.
No Israelite dared face this man
Till David came along.

He stepped up bravely, sling in hand,
He bore no sword or shield.
He felled Goliath with a stone
Upon the battlefield.

The enemy were terrified,
They turned and ran away.
They saw that God was with the boy –
Who would be king one day!

Jonah and the Big Fish

Once Jonah climbed aboard a ship
And tried to run away –
Though God had set a task for him
He dared to disobey.

God saw him flee and sent a storm.
The boat tossed to and fro.
Jonah knew it was his fault
And told the sailors so.

He made them throw him overboard –
The storm stopped there and then.
As Jonah sank into the depths
A big fish swallowed him.

Inside the fish for three whole days
He thought about his task.
"I'm sorry, God," he said, ashamed,
Then did as God had asked.

In the Lions' Den

Now Daniel lived in Babylon,
In exile from his land.
The king there grew to trust him and
Put Daniel in command.

But other men were jealous and
They set a trap for him.
They made a law that none may pray
To any but the king.

When Daniel still did pray to God
They made him pay the price.
Guards threw him in a lions' pit
In which to spend the night.

But God saved Daniel from the lions:
The king, amazed, did say,
"Your God deserves respect and praise
For what he did this day."

The Brave Queen

King Xerxes, angry with his wife,
Was seeking a new queen.
They sent for girls across his lands,
The fairest to be seen.

Young Esther was amongst the crowd:
The king chose her to wed.
Though Esther was of Jewish birth
Of this she nothing said.

Cruel Haman hatched an evil plot
To wipe out all the Jews.
But Esther bravely told the king
About his wicked ruse.

Though Haman's plan could not be stopped
The king did then decree
That Jews could now defend themselves —
They did — successfully!

A Baby in a Stable

Now Mary had been told that she
Would bear a special boy:
The Son of God this child would be,
He'd fill the world with joy.

Soon she and Joseph travelled far,
They went to Bethlehem.
The inns were full, a stable was
The only place for them.

That night the baby boy was born
'Midst cows and hens and sheep.
Then in a manger filled with straw
They laid him down to sleep.

In fields nearby some angels came
To bid the shepherds there
To visit baby Jesus, and
Tell people everywhere.

Following a Star

In distant lands three wise men had
Been studying the sky.
They knew a baby had been born,
A mighty king on high.

Across the hills and deserts dry
They travelled from afar.
At last they came to Bethlehem
By following a star.

They knelt before the little boy
And gifts they gave to him:
Sweet frankincense and gold and myrrh
All worthy of a king.

The years passed by and Jesus grew
A good man – kind and strong.
Now ready to begin the task
For which he had been born.

Fishing for Men

Now Jesus preached in Galilee
To crowds who came to hear
The scriptures he explained to them —
He made it all so clear.

One day he boarded Simon's boat
So crowds could hear him preach.
The fisherman was as transfixed
As those upon the beach.

And later Jesus told his friend
To drop his nets once more.
So many fish were caught in them
Though he'd caught none before.

The fishermen were all amazed
And left their nets right then
To fish for men with Jesus, and
To spread God's Word to men.

The Sermon on the Mount

So many people came to hear
What Jesus had to tell.
One day, forced from the synagogue,
A hill did just as well —

"How happy are the poor, the meek,
The hungry and oppressed,
Though life on earth is hard for them
In heaven they'll be blessed.

"Please understand, it's not enough
Just to obey God's laws,
Don't judge your neighbor, or stay cross:
Forgive him all his flaws."

He spoke of kindness and of love,
He showed them how to pray.
He taught them very many things
Upon the mount that day.

The Lost Son

Now Jesus told so many tales
(Parables they're called)
To help his listeners understand
The message they were told.

"A boy set out from home one day
To seek a life of fun,
But soon all his inheritance
Was well and truly gone.

He sank so low, he worked with pigs:
Ashamed he went back home.
His father welcomed him with joy –
No blame at all was shown.

He told his jealous older son,
"I hope you understand –
Though I love you, your brother once
Was lost and now is found."

The Good Neighbor

"A Jew when travelling down a road
Was robbed and left for dead
By thieves who after beating him
Stole all his things and fled.

"A priest and then a Levite both
Walked past him where he lay.
Choosing to avert their eyes
They went upon their way.

"A Samaritan then came along:
No friend to Jews was he.
But he knelt down beside the man
And helped him tenderly.

"So who's your neighbor," Jesus asked,
"The man who lives next door?" —
Let's offer help to anyone
Who's lost or hurt or poor.

The Healer

Soon people came from miles around
Amazed at what they'd heard.
The blind, the crippled and the sick
Were healed with touch or word.

Some men brought Jesus their sick friend
To see what he could do.
The crowds surrounding Jesus meant
That they could not get through.

Not giving up, a hole they made
Within the roof, and so
They could lower him on a mat
To Jesus down below.

"Your sins are all forgiven, friend,"
Said Jesus to the man,
Who jumped straight up, gave thanks to God,
Then out the door he ran!

Five Loaves and Two Fish

Soon evening fell but still the crowd
'Round Jesus would not leave.
They hung on every single word
Though food they now did need!

Disciples went to search for food
So that they could be fed.
They only found a boy with two fish
And five loaves of bread.

Then Jesus thanked his Father and
He tore the bread apart.
With baskets they passed through the crowd
And handed it all out.

Everybody ate that day
And there was food to spare.
With God's help little became much
With just a simple prayer.

Calming the Storm

As Jesus slept upon the boat
Tired out from all he'd done,
Dark clouds then passed across the sky:
A storm had just begun.

Wild winds came howling, rain poured down,
The waves were vast and high.
His friends woke Jesus, filled with fear,
"Please save us!" they did cry.

Then calmly Jesus looked at them
And on the bow did stand.
He faced the driving wind and rain,
"Be still," he did command.

The storm then ceased when Jesus spoke
And all around was still.
His friends in awe said, "Look, the wind
And waves obey his will."

A King's Welcome

Jerusalem was packed so full
For Passover was here.
And many came to celebrate
This special week each year.

Then Jesus on a donkey to
Jerusalem did come.
The people rushed to see him there,
They'd heard of what he'd done.

They threw down palm leaves on the ground,
"Hosanna!" they did cry,
"How blessed is the king of Jews!"
Their voices filled the sky.

But Jesus knew these people soon
Would sing a different tune:
He knew they'd turn against him and
Betray him all too soon.

The Betrayal

Judas, a disciple, sold out
Jesus for a fee.
For thirty silver coins he told
The priests just where he'd be.

While Jesus prayed upon a mount,
His friends close by his side,
Some guards and men came rushing in,
But Jesus did not hide.

To Judas who came forth he said,
"How has it come to this?
I know what you are here to do –
Betray me with a kiss."

Dragged off and questioned, Jesus then
Was brought before a crowd:
"Crucify him! Kill him now!"
They shouted out aloud.

A Cross on a Hill

Golgotha stood outside the town,
A hillside bleak and grim.
There Jesus hung upon a cross
A thief each side of him.

"Father, please forgive them for
They know not what they do!"
Jesus cried out on the cross,
His love still strong and true.

Then darkness fell, though it was day,
And Jesus cried out loud,
"It's finished!" — and the earth then shook,
As wonder filled the crowd.

But this was not the end – for God
Had meant for this to be.
And Jesus soon would rise again
To reign eternally.

Jesus is Risen

They put his body in a tomb,
Set guards there night and day.
They sealed the entrance with a rock
To keep his friends away.

Some women came with oils and salves,
As tremors shook the ground.
They looked inside but Jesus now
Was nowhere to be found.

Poor Mary wept there quietly,
A noise behind she heard.
Then, "Mary," came a voice she loved —
She knew with just one word.

"Lord Jesus!" Mary cried in awe,
Both hopeful and confused.
And Jesus spoke then, lovingly,
"Now go and spread the news."

Thomas Doubts

Now in a room had gathered the
Disciples late one night,
When Jesus suddenly appeared
And filled their hearts with light.

Only Thomas was not there
And doubtful he did grieve.
But later Jesus came again
And Thomas did believe.

"Now, you believe because you saw,
But blessed indeed are they
Who trust in me but need no proof!"
To him did Jesus say.

The time had come for Christ to leave
He bid his friends goodbye,
And then before their very eyes
He rose up in the sky.

A Special Gift

But Jesus promised when he left
That God would send a gift.
He knew his friends would need some help
And that he would be missed.

And as they waited patiently
The Holy Spirit came,
And landed on the head of each –
A single flickering flame.

They then could speak in languages
They did not know before.
By this they knew it was now time
To do God's work once more.

They went outside, spoke to a crowd
Of men from foreign lands.
And so God's message spread that day
For all could understand.

Paul Sees the Light

An enemy of Christians,
Paul chased them day and night.
But one day on his travels he
Was blinded by a light.

In fear Paul fell upon the ground,
Afraid at what he'd seen.
A voice from heaven spoke his name,
"Paul, why are you so mean?"

"Who are you?" Paul asked in fear,
Though deep within he knew.
"I am Jesus," said the voice,
And told him what to do.

Paul stayed in town and prayed for days,
He knew the voice was right:
His mind and heart were changed at last
For he had seen the light.

Spreading the Good News

And Paul became from that time on
A teacher of God's Word.
He spoke to people, and their lives
Were changed by what they heard.

He travelled into foreign lands
To spread the truth around.
Both Jews and Gentiles heard him preach:
He spoke to all he found.

At last he felt that he must go
Back to Jerusalem,
Although he knew his enemies
Were waiting there for him.

Set up, arrested, thrown in jail,
His faith he did defend:
A steadfast servant of the Lord
Until the very end!

Letters of Love

Though Paul was now in prison he
Did not give up the fight.
He wrote to those he'd met abroad
To show them what was right.

"You find things hard, but Jesus came
To free us all from sin.
Your rules won't bring you close to God
So just have faith in him."

He told his friends to work as one,
That each must play his part:
"None matters more than all the rest,
We're equal in God's heart.

"Don't mind the hardships that you face
For they will make you strong.
And trust you'll find your true reward
In heaven before long."